THE VALLEY PRESS ANTHOLOGY
OF YORKSHIRE POETRY

The Valley Press Anthology of Yorkshire Poetry

edited by

MILES SALTER &
OZ HARDWICK

Valley Press

First published in 2017 by Valley Press
Woodend, The Crescent, Scarborough, YO11 2PW
www.valleypressuk.com

First edition, first printing (April 2017)

ISBN 978-1-908853-73-8
Cat. no. VP0091

A CIP record for this book is available from the British Library.

Cover and text design by Jamie McGarry.

Printed and bound in the EU by Pulsio, Paris.

Contents

Introduction

If there is a county that can be regarded as the home of British poetry in recent decades, then Yorkshire's got a good chance of claiming the title. It has the advantage of being the biggest county in the UK, and has encompassed Humberside since 1996. The list of poets associated with Yorkshire is impressive: Ted Hughes, Philip Larkin, Simon Armitage, Andrew Motion, Roger McGough, Douglas Dunn, Carol Rumens, Sean O'Brien and many more have all resided, at least temporarily, in Yorkshire (often drawn to Hull). Ian McMillan has, from Barnsley, taken trains all over the country to broadcast, perform and entertain, in the process inspiring his son Andrew to become one of the leading poets of the younger generation. Helen Mort has used Sheffield as a place of inspiration, and Simon Armitage remains rooted not far from where he grew up in Marsden. Ian Duhig lives and works in Leeds. Pete Morgan lived and wrote in Robin Hood's Bay and York.

Today, Yorkshire is alive with plenty of activity in reading, writing and exploring poetry. In Sheffield (and, previously, Huddersfield), Peter and Ann Sansom have worked tirelessly at The Poetry Business, inspiring hundreds of enthusiasts. Carole Bromley's York Stanza group is one of the most respected in the country, with group members scooping many prizes each year. Antony Dunn has run Poetry Doubles, and subsequently Bridlington Poetry Festival, with a quiet but fierce passion. In Hull, Peter Knaggs has edited *The Slab*, while Shane Rhodes publishes via Wrecking Ball Press. In Scarborough, Jamie McGarry's Valley Press has provided opportunities for many up-and-coming and established poets to publish collections. Literature Festivals take place each year in Bradford, Ilkley, Sheffield, York, Beverley, Hull and many more locations, providing places where poetry comes alive through readings and workshops. Poetry groups across the county include Albert Poets (Huddersfield), The Red Shed (Wakefield), Writers in The Bath (Sheffield) and Otley Poets, to name a few.

This collection is not the only – or even the first – book to celebrate Northern or Yorkshire voices. What we've tried to do here is assemble some of the best contemporary poetry that is inspired by Yorkshire, often (but not always) written by poets currently based in the county. The poems reflect Yorkshire's varied landscape, from cities like Sheffield and Leeds to the rural life of the Dales. Broadly speaking, the book trips alphabetically around the county – with Barnsley and Bradford appearing early on, and York featuring towards the end. We have actively sought poems from some of the poets we admire, but also explored the hundreds of submissions received from writers around the UK. The results run the gamut from grave to frivolous. Death makes an appearance (which poetry anthology doesn't have a nod of the head to our mortality?), but so do football, friendship, Yorkshire puddings, and all the places where life's joy and mundanity are encountered. Carol Ann Duffy's 'Telephoning Home,' for instance, was inspired by seeing a man using a payphone at York station in the days before mobile phones. In their poems, Peter Sansom and Helen Mort explore areas of Sheffield, while John Siddique hunts down the location that inspired *Wuthering Heights*. Ian McMillan celebrates Yorkshire puddings. Stuart Pickford enjoys one of Yorkshire's big moments from recent years: the Grand Départ. Janet Dean thinks she spots Brian Jones (from The Rolling Stones) in Barnsley. Carole Bromley peers at The Stonegate Devil in York. Yorkshire is a place of amazing contrasts and variety, and this is reflected in the poems gathered for this anthology. All of life is here.

Our thanks to all of the contributors, and to Jamie McGarry for seeing the potential of the project.

Miles Salter and Oz Hardwick, York, February 2017

A Yorkshire Alphabet

Allotments, alleyways and arguments.
Bairns, Brontës, bowls and bitter.
Coal, cricket, caps and clubs.
Doms, darts, dogs and dales.
Eyup! Eyup! Eyup!
Football, fog, fags and ferrets.
Grudging, grim and gritty.
Headingly, Hockney, Hull.
Aye lad, aye lad, aye.
Jet, jam and Jessies (all southerners).
Keighley, khazi, Captain Cook.
Leadmines, leeks and liquorice.
Misers, moors and Mytholmroyd.
Nay lad, nay lad, now't.
Orkward, orkward, orkward.
Puddin's, pits, pints and pigeons.
Quakers, quoits and querulous.
Ridings, rain and Rievaulx.
Stubborn, stubborner, stubbornest.
Tea, Truman, tripe and terriers.
Unrivalled, unrivalled, unrivalled.
Vistas, Vikings and viragos.
Wolds, whippets and Wetwang.
X is what I put on me pools coupon every week.
Yokels, yorkers and Yorkshire Evening Post.
Z. Now what bloody use is that, eh?
We eat fish and chips up 'ere, not pizza, and
there's no Z in Barnsley, is there?
Think on, then.

Dave Gough

Heading North

The land sits lumpy, scuffed
like pelts on upland cattle
wintering out. A country
for bad weather, its hide thick,
toughened by shortening days.

The train's too fast for catching names,
though *-stone* must play a part, and *-field*.
The bridges have a solid, four-square set
about their jaws, and mortar sitting proud –
gritty assurance that they're built to last.

It's blackened land, even without the pits
and pithead spoil, and chimneys coughing dust
and smoke to oil the factory gates
that acid rains have scarred to rust.
The sun goes early, gratefully,

and leaves a scattering of lights
high on a spine of hill, until
another city starts its glare:
the B&Q, the car-park sprawl, the bits
that don't fit, could be anywhere

except they're here. Fast-forward. Leave the train,
feel Sheffield wind crisping the streets,
a cleanness on its breath, an eagerness
finding its feet to stamp across the maps:
whatever's going to happen's starting. Here.

D A Prince

Broken Biscuits

Is there poetry in broken biscuits? Discuss. The short answer is *yes,* provided it is articulated in the unashamedly Yorkshire, tongue-in-cheek, twinkle-in-the-voice tones of Ian McMillan of The Verb. You need a risk assessment now before being allowed to step onto a soapbox: its size, the maximum weight of poet it may carry. There is the marshal in a fluorescent jacket, carrying a walkie-talkie, clipboard and stopwatch, holding at bay some members of the Society for the Prevention of Cruelty to Biscuits. Biscuits are indexed and cross-referenced, generic categories and brand names listed: *Bourbon, broken, chocolate, chocolate (milk), chocolate chips, chocolate digestive (Milk Chocolate & Orange Digestive), digestive, dunking...* Specifications are laid out, spelled out and laid down for the packaging of biscuits. Here the blue and orange house colours of McVitie's nestle up with the listing of the ingredients: wheat flour, dried whey, cocoa mass, along with emulsifiers (soya lecithin, E476, natural vanilla flavouring), raising agents (sodium bicarbonate, ammonium bicarbonate, tartaric acid, malic acid). A touch then of the barbarous, barbaric, acidic and malicious. *Raising agents* might be the euphemistic title for these officials. Some Government-funded scheme would have lifted people off the scrapheap in a cold and distant Northern town; the group photo – five of them smiling in their smart uniform – appeared in the *Echo,* and now they do their daily rounds: moving beggars along, breaking up groups of young men loitering, or giving the impression that they are, or might be soon. The faded *For Sale* signs creak in the windy cave of a shopping mall, windows are boarded up and people – young girls in anoraks, smoking, pushing their friends; pensioners with stick and Zimmer frames – queue up in *Penny and Pound* shops for bags of broken biscuits.

Fokkina McDonnell

Haiku found in Barnsley

Walkabout Bar seeks
Part-Time Weekend Bar Staff –
No Muppets or Princesses.

Matt Black

Brian Jones

I remember the day;
a school trip to Lincoln,
the rippled whisper
they'd found him dead.
It made me sad
to think of him
floating face down
but when I met him
in Barnsley Market
a week or two later
he was cheerful,
smiling
in a way you wouldn't imagine
from the stony concentration
of holding his guitar neck;
but there he was, on the cheese
stall in his khaki overall,
his name embroidered
as proof,
his long slim fingers
spread across the marble slab,
his hand pulling tight and slow
on the cheese wire,
teasing the Cheddar
into see-through slivers
with the skill
of a true musician.

Janet Dean

Barnsley Boundary Walk – Over Woodhead

It's not a place for plimsolls, or flip-flops,
yet the red, hyphenated line squiggling
across the page makes it look an easy
ramble along an ancient bridleway.

Langset to Dunford Bridge, over a flat
patchwork of moor, ignoring the contours.
It beckons a rucksack full of sandwiches:
a hot flask, chocolate for emergencies,

cargo pants stuffed with wet-wipes, tissues,
aspirins, and a pocket full of loose change
for a pint of best bitter at the end.
The reality is, I am straddling a bog,

a living Colossus of Rhodes, carefully
moving, clump to clump, over a peaty
mire, like Rombald's ghost slogging home, my head
ramming into the blustery north west wind.

There's a thrum of traffic in the distance,
growling up Woodhead, masked by a howling
gale force. My waterproof jacket inflates,
a hovercraft's skirt, ready to move me

over the tussocks of tufted hair grass.
And, high in the sky, an eye watches,
waiting for boots to squelch into quagmire,
for oozing mud to trap me in a fold

of Gallows Moss. On the rise, a sharp shriek
tugs me backwards, gets inside my ears, reins
me in. I can see the chain on the page
meander past Windleden Resevoir,

I can feel it bruise my ankles. The eye
still watching, waiting, pins me to a patch
of purple heather, and in the distance,
a sign points to the middle of nowhere.

Jane Sharp

Immaculate

Before Madonna and the summer of sprouting body bits,
before comparing breast buds and wondering if
I'd develop conical tits instead of a comical
scribble of pubic hair and malleable mammary discs,
I entertained myself one day when I had time to fill
with Tiny Tears in a kind of mummers' play.
And I remember well, wearing my favourite
dungarees, pink the shade of bubbly-gum, button fronts,
and the buttons each had twins, buttons in reserve, back-up
fastenings for when I popped one off (I still have it in a tin
somewhere, faded to a softer blush that only hints
at the trauma suffered). That midsummer's day,
I took myself off down the back yard, laid
on my back under the left (as viewed going down) privet
bush of the pair outside old spinster Machin's window
to perform on the earth covered in clippings
a miracle birth where the doll was born breech
from the pinny of my dungarees. Being so hindered
by my clothing, it took some effort to extract
the infant, a trial pocked with ample groans, wails
and epic panting, succeeding at last
with an almighty yank. And it would have passed
unnoticed, marked only by the thread
outwardly probing like the filiform antennae
of the bugs thereabout where my button detached,
but for the spinster having watched it,
witnessed from of all places her kitchen,
as she put it to my mam: "Your lass,
making babies in the privet." Shaming me in the act,
dragging me back, she expected to see me slapped,

belted, leathered, tanselled, slippered, smacked
perhaps, but mam laughed, only
afterwards giving me a backhander
because I had been rolling in the dirt.

Rachel J. Fenton

with child

before my birth   my mother walked with concrete
animals   two hours before that she'd pulled
into the hard shoulder   a headache boring
through her skull   nine months before that   she'd made
tea   heavy with the weight of knowing something
had been done   sitting to eat as tension misted at the windows
and one morning   having carried me almost
full term my mother sat up in bed   saying
with an uncommon strength   that they had to drive
north   to the park with the life-sized animal
sculptures   and she wouldn't say why   except
it felt right   the unborn son with the whole life
ahead   the animals who would weather better
live longer   and would still be there
when their warm-blooded relatives were extinct

Andrew McMillan

Praise Poem for Yorkshire Puddings

Light brown moon in a gravy sky,
Round O of delight on a big white plate.
Floppy as a vest if you get 'em out early,
Hard as a wall if you get 'em out late!

Alchemy of eggs and milk and flour,
Aesthetically gorgeous in a kitchen full of steam.
Cultural symbol with enduring power,
Perfect as a sunset, elusive as a dream.

All in the wrist to get air in the batter
As the shattered eggshells lie crushed like martyrs.
As it waits to grace your Sunday platter
The Yorkshire Pudding is the queen of starters!

Ian McMillan

German Girl

A portrait by Euan Uglow, whose banning from an Arts Council exhibition by Bradford Alderman Horace Hird made national and international papers in 1962.

German Girl's hands are braced on her ham-thighs
as if she's about to plunge down a log flume.
She's got no clothes on. My Great Uncle made them put her
in a locked room
when the Arts Council brought her to Bradford in 1962.
She stares at me now on Google Images,
chin up, eyebrows slightly raised,
basin of purposeful hair,
small breasts pointing off to either side,
the brown triangle of her pubic hair
the portrait's vanishing point.
Turns out she's actually Polish.

Google shows Great Uncle Horace as an owl
in round black glasses,
hand on the gold mace embossed with boars,
Mayoral medallion warm on the centre of his chest,
ram and goat entwined in a disc of gold.
"Pornographic," he said,
"Lascivious."
"It will corrupt families.
We don't want somebody to see it
and go do something unspeakable in the park."

His nephew married my Mother
the year the Yorkshire Ripper started carrying a hammer,
and women stopped walking on their own after dark.

He photographed me and my twin brother with no clothes on,
each birthday from when we were four until we were eight,
straining to stand straight, arms at our sides,
marble, tiny, uncertain soldiers.

My sister slowly puts the Polaroids
on my brother's salvaged pile of childhood photographs
like the winning cards in a game of snap
he still isn't taking part in
no matter how much he loses.

Photographs make memories
become another go down the log flume,
an unlocked room.

Kate Fox

A Bratfud Life

Bratfud born, Bratfud bred,
Bratfud clothes, Bratfud thread,
Bratfud shoes, Bratfud tread,

Bratfud raised, Bratfud fed,
Bratfud milk, Bratfud bread,
Bratfud taught, Bratfud read,

Bratfud fought, Bratfud bled,
Bratfud love, Bratfud led,
Bratfud ring, Bratfud wed,

Bratfud jobs, Bratfud shed,
Bratfud skint, Bratfud dread,
Bratfud debt, Bratfud red

Bratfud youth, Bratfud sped,
Bratfud waist, Bratfud spread,
Bratfud years, Bratfud shred,

Bratfud sick, Bratfud bed,
Bratfud end, Bratfud dead,
Bratfud gone, Bratfud fled,

Bratfud done and Bratfud said,
Bratfud stone on Bratfud head...
...Bratfud A to Bratfud Zed.

Nick Toczek

Bradford Ghazal

This city is sad to you, head-down and down at heel;
but linger, letting your eyes run quickly to the hills.

They are like a faithful lover walking before you,
the way made sweeter by the breezes of her hills.

Even the pavement beneath is honeyed; warm sheltering stones
are at your side. Chiselled faces come down from the hills,

the faces of demolition gangs, replacing City
Centre concrete with vistas, (then) adding two extra hills.

So Rome has its equal and more, but who's counting, when
you're out of breath from tackling another of those hills.

City life's a steep learning curve, so let me name them:
Scarlet Heights, Odsal Top, Horton Bank and Brownroyd Hill.

Come let's go then where the gods can better hear us, higher,
that much nearer to heaven, on top of Bradford hills.

Bruce Barnes

Brimham Rocks

These big rocks, top-heavy, once seemed sculpted by druids,
and even now the devices of numinous floods. Deep lands
sweep down like an intake of breath, and the sun licks around
rock edges, striking life from the ragwort nectar trove.

Trees always stood here, birch, alder and oak, as they did
over all of the hills. And here one day a lynx chased a sunbeam
shaken around by the wind over last night's flint-struck ashes,
and a buckskinned hunter paused on a rock, and watched.

Amina Alyal

Three Sonnets for South Landing, Flamborough

I

Though this may be my last bench, it will do.
Up against the cliff and looking out to sea
I sit, a sight of dog and husband, too,
Something I had never thought could be.
While I am here I cannot come to harm,
I've learned the present is a welcome state,
A flower vase hangs off one wooden arm,
And my back warms a brass inscription plate.
I thought I'd lost the sea, the wading birds,
The sweep of sand and rocks, the sense of awe,
But they returned and I have found the words
And with increasing age it all means more.
This may be my last bench, and it will do
To sit and watch, to write. At last speak true.

II

The sea is neutral as it ebbs and dies.
It has no feelings, love or hate for me,
And I am wooed by all that it denies.
It cannot be anything but the sea.
The benches I have sat on by the shore
With my stories, to let them float or sink;
The boats in harbour, birds on ragged air
I have witnessed, they do not stop to think.
I have spent all my life in making sense,
Finding patterns where there are none,
The tracks of feet on a sandy expanse,
Seen by one sun and then they're gone.
I am warmed by more than sunshine here;
The neutrality of sea. It does not care.

III

These blues once made my spirit soar and sing
Of sea and sky, spring to summer turning,
But that is my past. I no longer cling
To blues of beginnings, youth and yearning.
I sit benched here against the tide and watch
The old sea roar, the sprung flight of martins
For whom no moment is too small to snatch,
While their time on the cliffs is passing.
For my dreams are no longer youthful dreams,
And I grow older as the seasons move.
My pleasures have changed, as year-end gleams,
And there is little left for me to prove,
Though loving the blue of joy-filled morning,
I am flames and ash of sunset burning.

James Nash

Fountains Abbey

You would love
the ruin now –
its frosted lawns
and flame-red beeches,
that yew a steadfast green.

You would know
how there must be green
with red and gold,
find similes for leaves,
think nothing of it too.

You would pause
by the great arch window,
liken its shards of stone
to a shark's jaw
mounted on a wall.

You would ask
if I had a dog,
a house, a garden,
was I playing cricket,
had I found another girl.

You would see
the place in snow,
hear those rooks caw
from the tower, dark
against the evening sky.

You would look
at its pink and blue,
ask me to do so too,
then say it was time
we were going home.

Will Kemp

Nobody Hurries in Harrogate

Nobody hurries in Harrogate.
You can see the old ladies who patiently queue
for a nice tea at Betty's, with salmon and cucumber
sandwiches laid on a white paper doily.
The waiters are smart, *maîtres d'* never oily.
On sunny Bank Holidays, see them in rows
with their Queen Mother hats and their very best clothes,
talking cribbage and cruises, a grandson's first tooth,
or twilight romances remembered from youth,
days when children were kind and MPs told the truth –
nobody hurries in Harrogate.

Nobody scurries in Harrogate.
The colonel with brogues and magnificent whiskers
(and lace underwear that he's pinched from his sisters)
just ambles along with no sense of alarm
and a rolled *Telegraph* tucked up under his arm.
He raises his hat to the ladies who pass,
and he longs for his gin in an icy-cold glass.
How pleasant to live in a town so serene,
where no one's aggressive and nobody's mean
and even the toilets are fragrant and clean –
nobody scurries in Harrogate.

Nobody worries in Harrogate.
On slow Sunday mornings the folk congregate
to take leisurely breakfasts on shiny white plates
at the cafés and bars down Montpellier Hill
to the chime of the church bell, the ting of the till.
Unfurled Sunday newspapers tell gloomy stories –
the bedroom tax, Syria, UKIP and Tories –

but while there's still cricket and cream scones for tea,
while there's monarchy, gentry and Radio 3,
there's no need to be troubled: be happy, be free,
because nobody worries in Harrogate.

Andy Humphrey

Hull

It's like that bloke at the bus stop
with a carrier bag full of bacon
going along the queue. *Like bacon?*
Everyone says no. Even I say no.

I love bacon, but I tell a lie
8:30 in the morning at the crossing.

Eh mate, do you like whisky?
Yeah, but I got four bottles
for Christmas.
What about Smirnoff?

I tell him, I don't have any money
on me, right at that moment. *Fair enough,*
he shrugs. I don't tell him the truth.
I don't buy stolen goods.

It's one of those things you don't do,
like drinking milk in a pub.

Peter Knaggs

Hull as a Shakespearean Tragedy

The daggers are hidden on Gypsyville.
Somebody looms in the shadows behind
the betting shop, waiting to whisper

a word like 'knave'. The lovers
meet on Whitefriargate as Queen Victoria's
statue prepares a soliloquy above the bogs.

There's cross dressing on Princes Avenue,
a wedding is announced, then cancelled.
Bouncers loom at doorways, ghosts of

tattoos on their knuckles. The final act
is at Hull Fair, where enemies with jewelled tongues
chew freshly poisoned mushy peas

as they pass pristine Gypsy caravans
then leap from the Humber Bridge,
shouting their losses at the tide.

Miles Salter

A Yorkshire Princess

This proud bird parades no vanity.
She paddles her feet in the Humber,
muddies her dress to show she's working,
hard as they'll let her.
Breathing in, breathing out,
she's a great warehouse, a production line
for the conquerors of kings, of prejudice,
the very skies. A rich vein of heroes,
natural, adopted, each giving body
to the history of a vintage port,
where alien poets blend in and flourish.

This proud lass breeds 'em tough,
strong, in strange times,
where opportunity arrives in trickles
like cod and praise.
And it is clear, despite the uncertainty,
the suspicions, the ghosts of Trawlermen
that haunt her vanished streets,
she'll continue to grow, to adapt,
a Yorkshire Princess and her people,
firmly rooted.

Mike Watts

Christchurch, Ilkley

In memory of:
dead flies seduced into the curve
of the bandstand light; lilac and grass soft
before the cut; a couple from Florida
                    who visited that summer of 63;

empty time-soured milk bottles;
condensation and exasperation breathed onto window panes;
men who rested in these corridors
                    before moving on, elsewhere.

The woman lays her prayer mat to the east.
Comes *for the peace*, she says, intones orisons
in glaze-stained rivers while behind her the bound St Agnes
                    is burnished in glass.

In memory of:
whatever it was that was ripped off the wall;
the one who arrives every week too early for song;
those who do not know how to pray, the curdling
                    of their need.

Becky Cherriman

'K Town'

If you look down you'll miss the rows
of cash-for-gold and pound shops.
You won't be drawn to bargain stalls
and promises of three-for-two-
end-of-season-everything-must-go.

You'll take no notice of the pram
pushers, *Big Issue* sellers,
the cider-soaked outside the pubs.
Look down – you'll only see the dog
belonging to the homeless bloke.

There's so much that you'll overlook
if your head is bent; you won't spot
the monument to the War dead,
or the nineteenth-century stonework
on the library. You won't see smiles

on the market traders' faces
or realise that what they sell's
worth looking at. Oblivious
of what you'd see if you looked up,
you'll walk on with your shoulders stooped.

If you looked up you'd see the moors
and the top of the green-tiled Mosque.
You'd see the mix of East and West
and young and old – you'd even see
that some of us call this place 'home'.

Gill Lambert

Nothing Pie

When I told my Dad that the locals called
a dandelion an 'Irish daisy',
I'd have to admit he looked disenthralled
so soon his farts were 'Yorkshire nightingales',

a dandelion a 'Yorkshire daisy',
a 'Yorkshire screwdriver' banged in his nails,
Tipperary invented the 'riding'
and 'Nothing pie' meant my Yorkshire pudding.

Abide with me, Daddy. Be abiding.
Now Owen's asking what our garden grows,
'bud' and 'good' full rhymes when he says 'budding'.
Mam will know. I call everything a rose.

Ian Duhig

The inter-species dialogue of Columba palumbus

We commune with children in Roundhay Park;
and old men with time in their pockets:

their sudden runs and jerked laughter;
their overcoats and paper-bag crumbs

are messages heavy with Loiner philosophy
and we join the debate with our tonal coo-cooing,

our head-bobbing, the exact way we strut.

We circumnavigate your air, write our white
hieroglyphs on the columns of Temple Works,

eat the crinkle-cut chips you proffer
in a precise order that speaks volumes

of our multiverse roosts, of the iridescent
galaxies to which we fly when Millennium Square

kicks out your last drunk, and the Civic Hall's
golden clock tocks past 3am.

Char March

Roads

I won't tell you about Waincliffe Place, the childhood days of one-handed skipping, the day the wind took my father, and the years of emptiness where a third plate, a third cup should be.

I won't tell you about Back Lane, where I took the dog for a walk every day, away from the prying eyes of strangers and neighbours, pretending the world belonged to me.

I won't tell you about Crow Nest Lane, where my primary school reigns supreme, with a panoramic view of the city, is the place that still haunts my dreams: I'm always running away.

I won't tell you about St. Anthony's Road, the happiest school-hood years, the odd best friend was found to confide in, writing short stories, avoiding the bullies, last to be chosen in games.

I won't tell you about Gypsy Lane, dread and fear on the way to the school of bullying, boredom and tears, looking over my shoulder, afraid of big girls, afraid the scars will bleed for years.

I won't tell you about Park Lane, where I hoped the bus would forget how to travel, how I discovered the lies of boys, the depth of friendship ties, and amazing A-Level passes.

I won't tell you about Old Lane, how my friend's mum got knocked down and could never walk again, and the post office that got robbed, and the waiting hours for the number 74.

I won't tell you about Cardinal Road, the windiest street there is, the wider spaces between houses, spaces between cultures seeming smaller, languages finding variant harmonies.

I won't tell you about Thirlmere Drive where my dog walked me as I dreamt unlived lives with my invisible twin brother, witnessed fields turn into business parks.

And I certainly won't tell you about Spring Avenue, where I lived before school set in, and how I remember the scent of pine on my fingers, the woman still shouting at me.

Bethany Rivers

Queen's Square

That strange lull between Christmas
and the start of the New Year
when nothing ever happens except rain.

Head down I cut across the square –
the Black Prince pointing from his horse,
his torso awkward, swivelling

with water streaming down his armoured back.
On the platform, counting down,
my last train stood, about to leave.

Coloured lights strung the periphery
or hung suspended from the massive tree.
I felt a tugging at my sleeve

and saw a ragged half-familiar face
under the lights, pressed close, the sack
of some grey hood around his neck

but fading quickly back into the crowd
like someone sinking in the sea,
wide eyed and looking up to find some hope

but finding none and letting go
holding on just long enough
to say *Don't you remember me?*

Ian Parks

Suburban

The day that him-over-the-back
leaned over his good fence and said
that someone in the night had dragged
a garden chair against the boards,
to vault through our tree's disorder
and trespass across our borders –

the day we paid a bloke to hack
the hawthorn hedge we later heard,
from her-across-the-way, had wrecked
her views, for years, across our yard
and down to where our suburb cedes
to the next grey ward into Leeds –

was the day we solved the tracks:
we drove home late and by the drive
our cats faced down a brace of fox
in the arena of our lights
in the run between the common
and our street of ransacked wheelie-bins.

They were not fighting and they were
not hackled up, and we unlocked
and locked ourselves indoors and saw
them deadlocked from each room we blacked.
And now we cannot tell how deep,
how fast, how still we are to sleep.

Antony Dunn

Mary Bateman's Lament

Mary Bateman, the so-called Yorkshire Witch who lived in Leeds, was hung in 1809 for murdering Rebecca Perigo by poisoning. She had led a life of petty theft and con tricks, one of which was a hoax involving a hen predicting the end of the world by re-laying eggs on which Bateman had written prophecies which the credulous paid a penny to see. Her body was publicly "anatomized" in Leeds and strips of her skin were sold to the audience as charms. Her skeleton was only recently removed from display.

I: THE PROPHET HEN

The sun will suck light from your eyes;
the moon will hang bloody in your sky.
Things slip backwards in these dark days;
naught is as it seems, and I, a simple
farmer's daughter, am become midwife
to doomsday. Look, my prophet hen
spells it out clearly – "Christ is coming".
It's a providence: each resurrected egg
a testament to our undeniable fate.
Pay me now; the end times are never late.

II: THE GATES OF MERCY

Gypsies skilled me in telling the future
but I did not foresee this fate for me.
I fed to the poxy Perigos white mercury salts
in honeyed pudding, for cure not murder.
All know me, a cunning woman with recipes
and remedies, potions against possessions.
It will not do; famed throughout this town,
yet twelve gawping men see only sorceress
or slut. They huddle quick, bestow the gallows;
the gates of mercy close, wreathed in shadows.

III: MARY BATEMAN'S LAMENT

Child, this day, as you sleep, I will hang.
I pleaded my belly to escape the scaffold
until a crone jury poked that to a lie.
I am to die; there can be no charm in that.
The Ordinary prevails on me to confess,
that compassion not given here may be found
beyond the grave. I will not trick any more.
No poisoner, but a thief whom no angel will save
from the drop when I must dance as a demon.
Remember me, daughter, a mere striving woman.

Patrick Lodge

Boar Lane, Leeds (1881)

after the painting by Atkinson Grimshaw

In those days shop windows meant business – just look
at the stonker for Taylors the Tailors: the Old Curiosity Shop
on steroids or laudanum, certainly. Even the upper floor panes
seem inflamed with assistants' ambitions, the friction of string,
motion of adding machines – and thank heavens it's siling it down
again: Boar Lane glitters like Blea Tarn or Scarborough.
Nobody's looking out over the roofs to an age
where the smoke and the glory and half the young men disappear
or beyond that, to one where the shops themselves shrivel
to matterless thoroughfares, paperless offices, weightless cash –
so let's button our greatcoats, galoshes and gloves, shake off
the kerchinging of cast-iron tills and step with young Grimshaw
and his century into a river you can't step into twice.

Julia Deakin

Cup Final

He collapsed
on the cold bare stairs
coming out of the stand.

They loosened
his blue and yellow scarf –
Leeds till he died.

His flat cap was pocketed
for a funeral cameo.

Flanked by sons, freaked
by the snap decisions of death
and lured by the familiarity of home,
he was propped up on the front seat
of the coach.

And all the triumphs of the years
were filters for his memory:
marriage to his sweetheart at 20,
crumbling seams buckling pit props,
back to back Wembley finals.

Cans stayed inside carrier bags
and songs of victory inside throats.
It's such a long drive home, they said.
It would've been how he wanted to go.

Neil Clarkson

Town Hall Steps, Leeds

Current thinking tells us that all time
is happening all the time
and though I can't really get my head around
this idea, it does occur to me as I eat my sandwiches
sitting on the Town Hall steps, busying a flake of old confetti
with my shoe, that if this current thinking is indeed true,
it means that while a couple kissed on these steps yesterday,
a man, right beneath their feet, added up the minutes
he would remain free. And it means that their marriage
could already
have been as long as his life was short, and that I was
disappointed
by my sandwich before the first bite, and that this bit of
confetti has always
been stuck to my shoe; evidence that thoughts move in circles:
reminds me days later of that man in his cell, that couple
out the door, and my place on the fringes of it all.

Jo Brandon

Chekhov's Gun

From a train, she passes how all things pass, wrapped
in their instants, messy and simple as the as-yet unlooked-at

complication, under the sign for a rail-station named
   Marsden –
which is like the surname of a first love, from

before I understood, like now – standing alone,
the inscrutable woman, all cheekbones

and short hair, and red polkadots rapped onto their white,
her hand raised to rest – perhaps briefly – against her cheek.
   Life,

for Chekhov, is neither horrible, nor happy,
but strange-unique-fleeting-beautiful-awful, according to
   Gerhardie

in this book I was reading before I shot by and saw the lee
of the sign for Marsden. *And for me, also* — and for me.

Joey Connolly

Gallows Hill

Gallows Hill is a nature reserve in Otley, West Yorkshire.
The last execution that took place there was in 1614.

Both children run ahead,
holding our personalities like balloons,
to build insect hotels
from hogweed and string.

A wilderness has grown
out of the printing mill's spoils –
surely only weeds will sprout
from this page?

Matthew Hedley Stoppard

Brinks

at Robin Hood's Bay

Neat as a scythe
The rain has sliced
A swathe of footpath from the cliff,
Discrediting the map.

Five hundred feet
Below that blackness where
The track goes over –
Into air –
The sea's tongue licks a thicket.
From here there's only one direction pulls;
Down, through an agony of gulls.

We lose a league of footpath every year –
It clicks off from the cliff's rim
Or it falls –
And year by year
The new rut where we cut our limit,
Inching closer to the hills,
Retreats no further from the sea.

There's something here
That sucks us to the brink
Like salmon homing in on home
Or moths round light,
Like the necessity to fight –
With no wars left, no common enemy –
Our own small wars of petty bitterness.

We test the strength
Of what we teeter on;
The brink of England or a love
Grown cold in that familiarity
Of who did what
To whom and why and when.
We go through this a hundred times. *Again.*

We need to know just where we stand, what odds
Are stacked against us by which gods
And what choice we have hidden up our sleeves –
To go on, give up, or avenge
The little wrongs that bubble with revenge.
Fear is the truth of this last limit where
The track goes over, into air…

Pete Morgan

An Opening at the Mill

A cosy café, a chic shop, a vast exhibition space
and now the glutted heavens are opening
at the old mill. The hills get a piece of the sky's mind

where Rousseau's tiger leaps as if lashed, imagined
beyond Hockneys and pale lilies quivering
in crazed Burmantofts. Apparently cavernous,

but the whole place seems to contract
to the shrinking lapse that separates strike
from roar. Staff tug at giant blinds

like riggers and, with each eye-splitting
flash, families with their transfixed children
become silhouetted, Victorian miniatures.

We were only just wondering about the sound
that must have once shuddered these rooms.
We'd asked a woman at the till

who came from a line of mill workers, whose
great-grandparents went completely deaf, both
cloth-eared at the loom– a world shrouded

where we sip our lattes and stare, not even
lip reading as they had learned, but silenced
except for the things only bones can share.

Rob Miles

In Scarborough

In Scarborough there's a grey seal
out at sea, a stack of dripping lobster pots,
a whelk seller wearing a woolly hat,
a nostalgia of postcards in a white rack.

In Scarborough the view is inside out with cold.
There is *In Memory of* and *who loved to sit here*
or *came to Scarborough every year.* There's a wind
that whips grass on the headlands, hats are lost here.

In Scarborough the word is: *funicular.*
There's a fuss and fluster as the season starts.
We've been huddled as gulls while the North
has been shut down. Now someone's fed the meter

and we can all begin again. In Scarborough
there's a curve to the *Valley Bridge* suicide rail,
there to keep us safe from ourselves. We jump,
in Scarborough, with the sea in our face. In Scarborough

there was a statue of Richard III: last king to reside
in our sea-scathed castle. There's an empty cage
where we thought we'd kept our history safe,
there's a space where he was, but he's been scrubbed off.

Wendy Pratt

Lowedges

And if those doors to other worlds exist

you'll find them here: Lowedges, where the city
smooths its skirt down in the name of modesty,

picks up its jacket, calls it a night. Here, bichon frises
chase their tails all morning on the astroturf,

a biker lets go of his handlebars and doesn't fall,
a woman rolls the afternoon into a cigarette

and smokes it silently. Forget the Cornish sea,
the top of Nevis with its trapdoor light…

If you're to leave this world, you'll leave it here:
this salvaged Friday, shop lights dimmed. Look up –

how easily the rain bisects the sky.

Helen Mort

Sheffield

When you arrive it is *far.*
In the wrong city the snow falls
like little shocks of other –
your knee-length coat
flapping open –

all day the buses move about the mid-eighties –
in cream and brown they stall at suburbs
with their tremendous and groundless names:
Intake, Herdings, Dore.

A dark afternoon. You find yourself
alone on the sixth floor of Sorby Hall –
a compass needle whirring in your heart.

Michael Brown

Seen in Sheffield

This is what boys are for! To strip
to the hip-sagging baggy pants;
shrug, slouch, then somersault to the brim
of the fountain; cat crawl the wall,
cartwheel, lazy-vault a stone plinth,
bend knees and flat foot it free-style,
frog-fashion, down all seven levels
of stone slabs sliced by blades of water.

This is what boys do: brace
on the handrail of city steps, spring
so that two feet lunge up to stand
on the next rail. Let go, drop back, land
squarely in size 12 trainers on the pavement.
Stroll back to the crowd, unflinching,
unsmiling, like no one's watching. Cool
as this cutting edge curve of water on steel.

This is what public sculpture's for: to mirror
these moves. This is what public spaces are for.
This is what this Saturday afternoon's for:
sliding down stone bannisters on one hip,
September not quite here. This
is what boys are: poems freed in air
above the sandwich wrappers in Sheaf Square
breakfalling among pigeons.

Cora Greenhill

Shalesmoor, Sheffield

Turning off eventually out of a jam,
I park up down the side street of another country –
Furnace Hill and Foundry Court, and Snow Lane in August,
all of it derelict to the point of grass on roofs
and willowherb gawping from what's left
of windows on this unguided walk. I look twice
at two girls with pints and a dog in front of no pub –
only Cook's (Bearings) Ltd (To Let) – and walk through
their 'He never was' 'he was' 'he never',
so oblivious they could be ghosts, or I could.
The shell of The Princess Works of Stavely Brass Co
dwarfs the prefab of Newland UPVC: then,
cresting Scotland Street, I come out at West Bar's
state-of-the-art cranes, high rise closing in
like combines flushing out the last wildlife
and razing the rare botany of die-cast and smeltings
down the pig-iron valley of yesteryear. I turn.
Yanks once touted the world's thinnest filament
to a firm round here, only to get it back
bored along its length. I like remembering that.
For answer, a carrier bag tumbleweeds past, startling me
and the girls and their dog no longer there.

Peter Sansom

You bought me a notebook at the Sculpture Park

and every blank page begins with snow,
our solid blue February sky.

Each paper turn is birdsong above frozen earth.
Even in a heatwave my fingers chill.

I write in ink that maps our tracks
past carved stone, long shadows,

by men, motionless,
our boots crunching prints in unison.

You bought me white space memories
we sculpted together, and a promise

to return when the lake is melted
and free to reflect the sky.

Fiona Ritchie Walker

Hare

The main crop in the East Riding is barley. Farming methods here have changed very little over generations. It is thought this might be why its vast barley fields have become home to the densest population of hares in the whole country.

Round Filey they say fishermen, on their way to work,
fear a hare will cross their path and bring bad luck,
their belief so fierce, they'll not put out to sea.
I love the hare who runs along late roads in front of me,
his black-tipped ears hearing what the moon sings.
Flecked fur springs and dips in my full beam mirroring
these Woldsian hills he's lord of. His strong back legs
overtake his front ones, spinning the world as he pushes
down like an Olympian breaking free from the pack.

The hare can turn on the petal of a daisy, part barley stems
then disappear between them to find his scooped form.
On mornings in the loving months, he's climbing the sky
to stand erect and box his future bride, show her, if only
she'll let him, how strong their progeny will be. *'Take me'*
each thrown punch requests of reeling air. She must be sure
he'll be as dependable as the promise in his eyes or
the full moon he's been known to leap to. Tonight, it seems
the stars have burst out in applause on learning she agreed.

Pat Borthwick

Vision From a Moving Car

Near Fridaythorpe
service station
on the A166

young woman bent
by the roadside
over a pram

ground-length hair on fire
sunset flaring
through it

husband or boyfriend
gazing away
smoking.

Robert Powell

From Kettlewell to Starbotton

Between the trees, white as bone, a cold sun shivers, a brightness
wavering, edging the leaf-fall with silver, the branchy rigging

stitched by skeins of honey-coloured fog. We trace the river,
follow its ascending breath through panes of light, through
hush.

We aren't lost, we've walked here long enough our boots
should know their own way back, rooted in decaying footsteps,

trekking through the cling and claw of mud, stumbling on snags
of ivy-root and twigs like snares, sleek tussock-grass, hard stub

of boulders, Wharfedale's 'stone hedgehogs,' shy ruckle
of moss in limestone crannies; our feet are pilgrims

steeped in the ritual of track and stile. From the fell's veiled
pulpit, a Dalesbred recites his sermon, low monotones to
summon

yowes. We trudge on. Small breezes charm the mist away, its last
rags
flitting, mothlike, through the trees, cobwebs like mantillas.

Lesley Quayle

Nidderdale

Back home, Alice made a nest of coats in the caravan she borrowed from a friend. She was off grid. It rained all night, Nidderdale rain, heavy and persistent, drumming on the metal roof of her box-shaped room, with the sound of the river like a bass note in the music of water. Her father would have remarked, *it's raining stair rods, lass* or *raining cats and dogs*. She thought of Escher's stairways leading nowhere, the Bourgeois print of a woman cradling an angry baby at the bottom of a flight of steps. At night she dreamt of stray terriers falling from the sky. Would she be *furred-in*, rather than snowed in? Limp, sodden bodies piled up against the cinder blocks of the caravan? Waking to sunshine was a relief. She parted the yellow beaded curtain and looked up to the grit-stone moors, birch trees shimmering like unspoken words.

Anne Caldwell

A Dalesman's Litany

He knows each inch and every half-inch of the land,
Each outcrop, every field, each stand
Of trees. His bailiwick, his kingdom – this is it.
He walks these windy acres with his stick

And dog. Stone-blind he still would know each wall,
Each field, by its own cry and call:
Wind songs in every tree, the voice of each small syke,
The babble of every spring and freshet, pool and dyke.

He is the last can read and parse this windy dale
(The fields and barns not named on any chart)
Yet draws back into silence like a snail
Under the salt of strangers' questions. He has the land by heart.

Schooled by the fells about, he hoards the rubric in his blood:
Fields, barns, crags – his lexicon, word book.
His gazetteer's not one you'd find in any guide or map –
Jaggers Way, Dub Foss, Dear Bought Wood,

Peacock's Barn, Lad's Rake, Burnt Syke.
From the twisted thorn in the limestone gryke
To the rowans in the outrake – his litany and bible,
Each gate and gap, each cripple hole and stile.

And when he goes the book will be no more,
The story of the land will sputter like a candle flame
Snuffed out, and all its legends, tales and names
Lost in the wind of the future's careless open door.

Mike Harding

Anatomy of a Landscape

'Found' element from OS map of Reeth High Moor

Whaw! Booze Common.
Little punchard.
Great punchard gill.
Gillhead moss.

Adjustment Ground or 'the Disputes'

Shaw tongue, tongue end;
dicky edge, little cocker,
cocker.
Great cocker. Cocker top.

Wetshaw bottom. Hungry hushes.
Fox hole, deer holes, shake holes,
swallow holes.

Slack wife gill, clay intake nook.
High whim (disused).
Thistle hill.

Surrender ground.

Hannah Stone

Le Grand Départ

Under a cherry tree flirting with sun,
we place our blanket in the Fan Zone;
the kind of morning pubs are open
all day as brass bands stir up a tune,

which they are and do. The town's
taken over by us, the locals, high-fiving
the police as we wander closed streets.
Never mind the Royals, we live here.

Some spectators muscle into a wedge
on the finishing line but we lay back
in shade, watching God's own county
unfold before us like a coffee-table book:

Bolton Abbey where we hopped across
the stepping stones on our very first weekend,
The Craven Arms where we settled on the name
Ashley, Grass Wood and its orchids.

Soon we're toasting The King of the Mountains
on the Col de Buttertubs where the crowd raves
across the road–and someone's dressed
as the devil, thinking it's the Dutch Corner.

Then fields mowed in the shapes of bikes,
sheep dyed yellow, red and white.
As the tour rounds Ripley with its grandstand
of straw bales, you jump up and make off

towards the road. As the crowd's ten-deep,
we do what we've not done in years.
You clamber up onto my shoulders, laughing,
and translate the race's French commentary

as the peloton nears. I can't see a thing
but can feel you shouting, *They're coming.*
They fizz past as you cry to Cavendish,
to all the riders and crowd, *Come on. Yes.*

Stuart Pickford

The Moor

The moors are empty, no one for miles around.
The wind has woven the grass through fence mesh
so that it's now quilted between posts.
There are ghosts here, echoes: the far off blue

of the reservoir, the sound of curlew, or a grouse
that batters the air as it jumps to something unknown.
There has never been anyone here. The cotton grass
shimmers in the sunlight, fields of silver white

crossed by cinder and stone. Shadows of clouds race
and the land flickers like an old film. Sometimes
you said, it's all we need to be. We are miles
from anywhere and I swear I can smell the sea.

David Coldwell

Saturday Jobs

Lunchtime, still hungover, I'd break off
washing cars and come to find you behind

the counter at the busiest bakers
in town. You'd pretend you didn't know me

and fill a larger carrier bag with rolls
and cakes, a couple of loaves to take home.

I'd pass you a five pound note and you'd give
me my change, five pounds exactly, in coins.

Michael Shann

Spell

Roaring morning; tide seemingly breaking against
windows, sea unfurling in greys and whites;
ferry pitching across, forwards and sideways.

Park with back to storm; salted car trembles.
Ferry bucks and rears, an unbroken seahorse,
to connect its ramp to slipway with clang and grate.

A quick loading in churn of judder and boiling,
slipway and deck awash as part of tide;
dropped passengers daring backwash, towing cases.

Then a surge leewards as everything backs off
into pitch of the Sound. A squall dared
to duck from parking lay-by into empty cottage,

and check: fee left on table with labelled key,
a 'Welcome to White Rose Country' tourist leaflet,
folder of local walks stowed back in bookcase.

And in the quietness before resuming
war with weather, unrolling long miles home,
a drawer is opened, moment, for a gift,

a pencil added to crayons and half-used biros,
lime green of springing pasture in Spring sunlight,
ram's head and caption Yorkshire National Park.

Turn to return. He'd check that drawer quite early
if he came back, small cylinder of limestone dale
left among yachting charts, and tartan throws.

Ready for sketching, shopping lists, postcard greetings:
'We waved it like a wand, and weather changed.'
Door left unlocked; ferry far out; gale easing.

Martyn Halsall

The Bellymen of Wakefield Town

An empty mime of creation, they grow no flesh
and bone, and they stand and they scratch in the mud
and gizzard as round and round roils the pot-bellied wizard.

They could be giants in the mansion trades
making houses, but for these beer belly masquerades,
raising buildings stick by stick, chanting,

'Grow this house brick on brick, and
make the cement stick fast and thick.'

Dusk-primed, they rip off their shirts and dance unafraid,
beer-fed bellies out at last, on parade, pot bellies roiling,
cement mixers toiling, on and on and pass the hipflask, primal
dances from the past, chants from the shadows to set and cast,

'Grow this house brick on brick, and
make the cement stick fast and thick.'

They suck their teeth and stomachs in,
sinking ankle-deep as the mud draws in, but the bellymen,
the bellymen, they shake their bull-necked heads and grin.

Sarah Wallis

Whitby

Whirlpools of gulls whip over harbour –
clouds of yellow eyes –
and the stone sea's fearsome, melted
and roused to terrible passion.

Adders slip through moors.
On the promenade lovers
masticate winkles.
Punch kills the baby.

The roses on the fortune teller's
tatty hut are leeched,
and I've never bought a reading
for fear she'd shrug,

for I am good and pure, a bore,
and in my room, again,
writing in this diary, its prim script:
today piano, teas, I walked.

I took in air.
I made small talk.
My engagement ring tightens;
a noose on the gallows.

Yet something dark veins me,
as jet veins these cliffs –
black crystals brought
to toughness by time's weight.

When the tourists see
the mourning jewellery,
I've watched their covetous eyes;
how they gleam. And a fire

catches in me.
I'm the lighthouse lamp,
guiding something in –
the bay's sand fingers strain –

and a prow pierces the beach –
and a dark beast slumps up steps
to the graveyard,
to the through-stones flat as beds,

the shuddering clouds,
the white moon like a fingertip
pressed up to glass –
a brute bat's wings are beating at the glass!

Come on then – I invite you in.
Why fight my own thought?
I'd roam this world too.
Penetrate it.

Feed on me that I can feed,
for I am sick of being tame.
Evil and freedom
are the same.

Clare Pollard

Postcard from Whitby

Goth toenails, hard as the jet on grandma's bosom,
sandalled bunions, hand-me-down Jellies, tap
tap tapping: all sucked down one hundred and ninety

nine steps, or slopes slippy with sand thrown by the sea
on exuberant days. Trippers grip a paint topography,
handrails whipped in the teeth, in the face, of the North Sea.

Human soup, sluggish along harbour walls,
tethered to dogs, pushchairs, gobstopper machines,
eddies round the 'A' boards of boat trip skippers,

settles on benches, any vacant concrete. Bare back
donkeys   munch lunch   twitch
their bony shoulders, their tracks a daily tattoo

the sea will tease, lick, wash into and away.
Oh look–the concrete ichthyosaurus
a fortune fish silent on the pier

to trip us into prehistory
as well as lost vanilla cornets, an end–
just someone's lunch. Armfuls of plump, clean seagulls

canny amongst toddlers and photographers
peel their chewing gum pink feet from the quay
then fall
          out over the tide   and soar

to the relief map of home where they tell you
I have seen couples who still touch each other's skin.

Carol Rowntree Jones

Wuthering Heights

54° 31" 25" N   2° 33' 49" W

The pale face of the sun backlights the horizons,
though cloud overtakes her to paint the land
in edges, dissolves and promises.

Wind quickly changing everything:
heat becoming cold, dark air shifting towards hope
and lightness coupled with a bar of shadow.

The moraines of a house have been lifted
from the mossy grave of the moor, for tourists
risking their footing, climbing after one story and another.

Finding an unripe bilberry patch below Wuthering Heights,
we riff off the tastes of rough jams and summer puddings to
come.
You sit where a young woman may once have sat
tonguing the corner of her mouth as she wrote.

Her husband waits to kiss her soft edges
when she breaks into her wide girl smile, relieved
after painting lines of poetry into her notebook.

I kiss you too, as you talk of sheep and jam, aware of
new ferns unfurling from the death of last year's growth.

We are only upright against the horizon for a time.
The lintels of the house at Top Withens have been reset.
Weather closes in over us, over the body of the hilltops,
over the ruts of sheep-grazed valleys.

John Siddique

The Riverside Arms

The landlord pulls a pint
and the foam surges
over the rim of the glass.

On the wall is a chart
of previous floods,
a living graph of how

Matt, in '31, stood with water
lapping at the heels
of his Wellington boots;

Cameron, in '45, sat
with his G&T, waist deep
at this warping table;

Susan, in '68, had to hold
her glass of white head high
to keep it dry;

and Michelle, in '82, finally
let that shot of Drambuie
slip from her grasp

into the rising tide
like a depth charge
and felt her earrings

tugged upwards
like buoys
or fisherman's floats…

In the following century
it's a different tale:
the barman dispenses

neat measures of scotch
and vodka from the optics
while the electric pump

drizzles beer to a thin line
that shows precisely where
enough is enough.

Paul Munden

Telephoning Home

I hear your voice saying Hello in that guarded way
you have, as if you fear bad news, imagine you
standing in our dark hall, waiting, as my silver coin
jams in the slot and frantic bleeps repeat themselves
along the line until your end goes slack. The wet platform
stretches away from me towards the South and home.

I try again, dial the nine numbers you wrote once
on a postcard. The stranger waiting outside stares
through the glass that isn't there, a sad portrait
someone abandoned. I close my eyes ... Hello? ... see myself
later this evening, two hundred miles and two hours nearer
where I want to be. *I love you.* This is me speaking.

Carol Ann Duffy

York Ghosts

We arrived nearly forty years ago,
when the dog-end of a real summer
got wasted by an autumn deluge.
It was another two weeks at least
before we could walk along the river
from Fulford, past Redfearn's Glass
then up Clifford Street into town.

Lowland mist permeated the narrow
lanes all the way round the Minster,
thickening into smoke-stained fog
with a seasoning of beer and beet.
Swaggering from our tutorial success,
albeit borderline, it wasn't so much
of a choice between food and text.

We may have been shocked at first
by those swarms of riderless bicycles
crossing Lendal Bridge at shift change.
The same applied to that call for best
of order in narrow public bars as darts
began to fly. Where daffodils lay siege
to the city walls, people rarely slept.

I spotted one Aitcheson cat on a wall
in Low Ousegate on my way home
from the Arts Centre, its perpendicular
territory brisk with rain. There was
a shortage of blood then – you needed
a private source if you wanted some
for drinking or sharing with friends.

Oliver Comins

The Stonegate Devil

He's seen it all: mummers, buskers,
guildsmen pulling carts with wobbling tableaux
of flood, famine, crucifixion;

a couple choosing a ring in Walker and Preston's,
a man hurrying another man's wife
down the alley to Ye Olde Starre Inne,

drunks vomiting in the snickleway,
the purple cyclist on his purple bike,
going nowhere.

The devil's crouched on that ledge
since Coffee Yard was Langton Lane
and Stonegate the Street of the Printers.

He doesn't need the gear in *Old Guys Rule,*
wears a black chain and a pair of horns,
his skin boiled lobster,

those hands on his knees a man's hands,
his feet the feet of a goat
and, though you can see his ribs,

he has no appetite for the eggs
in *Bettys* display, the chocolate otter,
the hare or the candy daffodils,

does not thirst for the spirits
in the window of Evil Eye
or the barrels in Trembling Madness

where the missing student on the poster
Megan, we would love to hear from you
smiles her pretty smile.

Carole Bromley

Newsworthy

York flood, December 2015

A dun tranquillity spreads
where yesterday the children
chased their cries and shoppers
on the concourse thumped
shut car boots.

Now, side by side, we look on,
ourselves and the world at large,
as the eventful happens
here, in our street – a vision of
drowning signposts, rows of houses
with the Buster Keaton stare
and what it must be like to be us.

Ian Harrow

The Travelling Salesman Raises His Eyes

York on a Spring afternoon, the air clouded
with coffee and baking: *Makes a change.*
Through the railings, two children – girls
in Disney dresses – play three-way tennis
with a young woman, probably their mother.
There's more running about and shrieking than
actual ball contact. Above, the stained glass window,
black from the outside, dates from the 1330s
and is crowned by the Coronation of the Virgin
and Christ in Majesty. *Spare change. Spare change.*
The rattle of coins in a plastic cup, and of a bell,
as a cyclist cuts a precise pastry-wheel arc,
changing gear as her legs stretch from brief inertia.
Spare change. The Great East Window,
by John Thornton of Coventry (early 15th c.),
is the size of a tennis court. *In my case,*
that opens to the scent of wood and wax,
my grandmother's kitchen, and the school bell,
I carry: twenty bright yellow dusters
with red stitched edging; eight 400ml tins
of furniture polish; six tins of Brasso;
three – *Watch where you're going, Mate!*
Languages I don't recognise, from countries
I'll never visit, sing together a liturgy of wonder,
as strangers renounce themselves, turn eyes upwards
to: tracery in the French curvilinear decorated style;
light cloud with bright spells later; *and, perhaps…*
heaven? The tennis players gather their belongings
and head towards the gate: there was no score. On cue,
a peal of bells, ringing changes.

Oz Hardwick

Unsteady

Sometimes you can feel the sand shift under Bachelor Hill.
Topped by a dozen pines like birthday candles
or now, in the dark, mad fingers that rake the moon,
the climb seems steeper than I remember.

Careful to avoid the side gouged by diggers –
sand so fine it streamed from their jaws like water –
then past the place I buried your letter,
I reach the top and look down on a town

turned in for the night, televisions bright,
someone cycling home under warming streetlights,
and I feel the same as when, slowing down
along a railway line at night, I look into the backs

of lit houses, and know what it's like to have
no grounds to be anywhere, suddenly envious
of the woman at the sink, the dog
tethered in the yard.

Doreen Gurrey

York Street Furniture, 1981

Colin says he's got to have a break:
he's gasping, and the bog's the only place
they let them smoke. He takes the Players pack
out of the pocket of his long, buff jacket.

I don't, but then he doesn't even ask.
We talk, but say nothing. The fifty quid
a week is college beer money for me –
for him, it's life-long beer money, perhaps.

And when the tab's half-done, the foreman slams
in, takes one look, says, "What the fuck?" and kicks
me out, for wagging off when I don't smoke.
I'm back to loading king-sized mattresses

myself. I try just one. Can't even span
my arms across, so I stand and sniff
the reasty, hot machine-oil air, sweetened
by seasoned timber, as it turns to sawdust.

Mike Farren

Tabernacles

Under the statues' stony gaze, beggars huddle
  at the kitchen door on Nunnery Lane.
Windows furred by traffic fumes screen cloistered rooms.
  Women genuflect on golden floors,
swish across the bloom of love on beeswaxed tiles,
  tend tiny mysteries of host and flame.
At four o'clock, girls in blue capes scatter like petals
  on Blossom Street, where buses wait,
Acomb, Tang Hall, Tadcaster, Wetherby
  – all the world and universe beyond.

Marie Naughton

Family Group at York Station

My jacket chafed, the collar too tight,
buttons pulling across my chest.
We stood stiffly, not yet parted,

but no longer together. Better to leave now
than wait, with Millie trying to be brave
and not daring to speak, and her mother

in her dourest chapel-faced black,
as if she were burying me already.
The photographer helped fill the space

between farewell and whistle.
We stood in line beside a stranger and his family.
It was cheaper to share. I never saw him again.

Maybe a bookcase in some northern town
shares us still, our last picture before
the whistle blew.

Pauline Kirk

Surviving the Prince of Wales

Sunk, 10th December 1941, South China Sea

You walked for hours, freed from cat-gut and applause, week
after week,
miles from your London house, your cap slanted, scarf pulled
tight, as if
a young lad homing back from school on heathered fells, over
the fields

through Calderdale to mother, sisters, tea, the kitchen range;
as if, straight after practice, still loping to the rec, to catch
the squeaky metal of the swings, or dizzy in the spin of solid
wood

that turned and thumped in any weather, conjuring a view
beyond the grey stone town, across to Holmfirth, Saddleworth,
or south to Ainley Top; long before the M62 rose and dipped
away

somewhere further than imagining – before the crazy ack-ack
and the roar, before the burning sea, mouthfuls of oil
and screams of mates betrayed aboard that ship; as if long
before –

you walked for hours, miles. Metal segs tapped out the route
between
suburban garden fences and post-war semis; your mind's eye
roved over crags and streams to the wooded sheen of winter
leaves

and silvery bark, to shadows draped on dry stone walls
and dales cresting blue into air; till your throat filled with chords
that beat your heart afresh, sweet pipe smoke trailing a tale of home.

Yvie Holder

The Gallery Tour Pauses in Front of Simon Armitage's Portrait

Smudged askance, we can't decide
if he's looking at himself,
already looking back, at twenty-eight
writing how he liked his filling-out of face –
or at what scenery seems to be behind,
the landscape he's to figure in.

Even as his dyke-wide shoulders
are rising, darkly, out of snow
he's thinking Marsden Caribbean,
lilac-lushened. Turquoise splashed
in verticals falls to make paradisical
pools of the Huddersfield canal.
Even what appears up-close
as the sage of Pennine grass
with grit-stone underlay
is turned tropical by a three-hour sitting.

Painter's abstractions of geology, weather,
defy an easy correspondence
with the fault-lines of the poet's face,
behind which he might be thinking
of war zones, famine, stuff
he mustn't forget to pick up on the way home
or, to pass the time while posing,
fixing a stanza, working out a line.

This painted smile's more rueful
than the one he verbalized
a couple of decades before.
Whatever's behind him,
jungle – indiscretion – moor
could stand for what's behind us all.

We read his words in front of him,
imagining some movement
by the corner of his lips,
sure he's just about to clear his throat.

Helen Boden

About the Contributors

Amina Alyal has been published widely, in academic publications and in journals and anthologies including *Dream Catcher*, *Envoi*, *Iota*, the *Aesthetica Creative Writing* and more. Her poetry collections include *The Ordinariness of Parrots* (Stairwell Books, 2015) and *Season of Myths* (Wordspace Imprint with Indigo Dreams, 2016).

Bruce Barnes is retired and recently graduated from the Writing M.A at Sheffield Hallam University. His poetry collections include *the lovelife of the absent minded* (Phoenix Press, 1993), *Somewhere Else* (Utistugu Press, 2003), *Israel Palestine* (Otley Word Feast, 2016) and *Out Of his Struggles – The Poetry Of Kosuke Shirasu* (Utistugu Press, 2016). His writing has appeared in numerous journals and anthologies.

Matt Black lives in Leamington Spa. Since being Derbyshire Poet Laureate (2011-2013) he has successfully completed over 20 commissions, with poems on 15 benches, 20 milestones, a large glass panel, and in exhibitions and publications. In 2017 he has a pamphlet (*Spoon Rebellion*) being published by Smith Doorstop, and in 2018 a book of travel haikus (*Tales from the Leaking Boot*) by Iron Press.

Pat Borthwick lives on the Yorkshire Wolds. She has four full length collections and several pamphlets to her name. She has received two International Hawthornden Awards. Competition first prizes include the Keats-Shelley, the Basil Bunting and the Ted Hughes Elmet Award. She teaches creative writing, leads a Stanza group and undertakes private mentoring and writers' residencies.

Helen Boden is a Yorkshire-born, Edinburgh-based writer, educator and editor, with poems in magazines and anthologies including *Mslexia*, *Butcher's Dog*, and *New Writing Scotland,* as well as artists' books and pamphlets.

Jo Brandon was born in 1986 and lives in West Yorkshire. Jo's pamphlet, *Phobia* (2012), and her debut full-length collection, *The Learned Goose* (2015), are both published by Valley Press.

Carole Bromley has published two full-length collections of poetry with Smith/Doorstop, most recently *The Stonegate Devil* (2015). She lives in York where she leads the local Stanza poetry group. Her work has been widely published and she has won many prizes for her poetry, including the Bridport Prize. A collection for children, *Blast Off!*, is published in 2017.

Michael Brown's work has been published widely, including *The Rialto, Lighthouse Journal, Other Poetry, Crannog, South Bank Poetry, Envoi, The Moth, The North, Brittle Star, New Walk* and *The Interpreter's House*. A pamphlet, *Undersong* (2014), is available from Eyewear Publishing. A short pamphlet about journeys by car and rail, *Locations for a Soul*, was published in autumn 2016 by Templar Poetry.

Anne Caldwell has published three collections and is widely antholgised. She was longlisted for the National Poetry Competition in 2015. Her current book of poetry is *Painting the Spiral Staircase* (Cinnamon, 2016). She has worked for the University of Bolton, NAWE and the British Council and now lectures for the Open University. She was shortlisted for the Rialto Pamphlet competition in 2017.

Becky Cherriman is a commissioned writer, workshop leader and performer based in Leeds. Her work is informed by the belief that not only do the written and spoken word help us make sense of the world and our place in it, they provide us with the tools to transform our lives. Becky's poetry pamphlet *Echolocation* and first collection *Empires of Clay* were published in 2016 by Mother's Milk and Cinnamon Press respectively. She is currently working on a one woman show.

Neil Clarkson is a long-standing member of the Albert Poets in Huddersfield. He has been published in magazines including *Pennine Platform*, *The Black Horse* and *Obsessed by Pipework.* He has won prizes in numerous competitions. His debut collection, *Build You Again from Wood*, was published in February 2017 by Calder Valley Poetry.

David Coldwell is an artist based in Marsden. His studio is perched at the corner of the Yorkshire Pennines. His debut poetry pamphlet, *Flowers by the Road* (Templar Poetry) is published in 2017.

Oliver Comins lived in 20th-century York for five years, some of them as an undergraduate. Templar Poetry has published three pamphlets in three years: *Yes to Everything*, *Staying in Touch* and *Battling Against the Odds.*

Joey Connolly lives in London, where he manages the Poetry Book Fair and edits *Kaffeeklatsch* poetry magazine. His poetry and criticism has appeared in *The Best British Poetry 2014* (Salt), *New Poetries VI* (Carcanet, 2015), *The Poetry Review*, *The Sunday Times* and on BBC Radio 4. He received an Eric Gregory Award in 2012, and his first collection, *Long Pass*, was published by Carcanet in 2017.

Janet Dean was born in Barnsley and lives in York. She was shortlisted in the Bridport Prize in 2012, and commended in the Stanza Poetry Competition in 2015. In 2016 she co-edited and launched *The Friargate Anthology* at the York Literature Festival. Janet has an MA in Creative Writing from York St John University, and has recently completed her first novel *The Peacemaker.* She is a member of York Stanza and a contributor to live poetry events in and around York.

Julia Deakin is widely published, has won numerous prizes and featured twice on Poetry Please. Her collections *The Half-Mile-High Club* (a Poetry Business competition winner), *Without a Dog* (Graft 2008), and *Eleven Wonders* (Graft 2012), are all authoritatively praised.

Carol Ann Duffy is the author of numerous collections of poetry, including *Selling Manhattan*, *The World's Wife* and *The Bees*. She is currently the Poet Laureate.

Antony Dunn was born in 1973 and lives in Leeds. His poetry collections include *Pilots and Navigators*, *Flying Fish*, *Bugs* and, more recently, *Take This One to Bed*. He is Director of Bridlington Poetry Festival where he has worked with many of the UK's leading poets. Antony runs Poetry School workshops in York and Leeds.

Ian Duhig has written seven books of poetry, most recently *The Blind Roadmaker* (Picador, 2016) which was shortlisted for the Roehampton, Forward Best Collection and TS Eliot Prizes. A Cholmondeley Award recipient and Fellow of the Royal Society of Literature, he has won the Forward Best Poem prize once and the National Poetry Competition twice. A former homelessness worker, he is currently writing a piece for *Refugee Tales*.

Mike Farren is a poet and editor in academic publishing from Shipley, near Bradford. His poems have appeared in *The Interpreter's House, Prole, Ink Sweat and Tears, Algebra of Owls, Leads to Leeds* and numerous anthologies. He is one of the hosts of the Rhubarb open mic in Shipley, and his debut pamphlet, *Pierrot and his mother,* will be available soon from Templar Poetry.

Rachel J. Fenton was born in South Yorkshire in 1976 and is currently based in Auckland, Aotearoa, New Zealand. Her poems have appeared in *The Rialto, Overland Journal, Poems for a Liminal Age,* an anthology in support of Médecins Sans Frontières, and she was runner-up in the Ambit 2016 Summer Competition, judged by Sarah Howe.

Kate Fox has made a living as a stand-up poet for ten years. Being funny and Northern is sometimes a help and sometimes a hindrance and she's doing a PhD about why. Sometimes they let her on Radio 4. Her car radio is tuned to Radio 2. *Fox Populi* was published by Smokestack in 2013 and *Chronotopia* is forthcoming from Burning Eye Books.

Doreen Gurrey lives in York, where she is a member of the local Stanza group. One of her poems was highly commended in the 2013 Bridport Prize.

Dave Gough lives and works in York. He is a regular contributor to live literature events in York, and has also performed at Beverley Folk Festival and Ilkley Literature Festival. Dave is part of the team that runs York Literature Festival.

Cora Greenhill's recent collections are *The Point of Waking* (Oversteps Books, 2013) and *Far from Kind* (Pindrop Press, 2016). Her verse drama, *Artemis, The People's Priestess*, comes out with Three Drops Press in April 2017. She has hosted Writers in The Bath, a poetry reading venue in Sheffield, since 2014. All this since she retired. She has lived spitting distance from the S. Yorks border in The Peak District for thirty years when not in Crete or Africa.

Martyn Halsall has worked as a journalist for *The Guardian*. His books include *Signposts To The Interior* (Crocus Books, 1998), *Sanctuary* (Canterbury Press, 2014) and *Coronach* (Wayleave Press, 2016). He was the first Poet in Residence at Carlisle Cathedral.

Mike Harding is a singer, songwriter, comedian and poet residing in the Yorkshire Dales. His career has encompassed recordings, performances and broadcasting. For many years he presented the BBC Radio 2 Folk, Roots and Acoustic Music show. He now presents *The Mike Harding Folk Show* via the internet. His latest book of poems, *Fishing for Ghosts*, is published by Luath Press.

Oz Hardwick lives in York. He is Professor of English at Leeds Trinity University. His interests include photography, music and medieval art. He is a regular contributor to *R2* magazine and the author of six collections of poetry. His latest collection is *The House of Ghosts and Mirrors*, published by Valley Press in 2017.

Ian Harrow's poetry has appeared in *The Times Literary Supplement, The Spectator, Oxford Magazine, Stand, Poetry Wales, Other Poetry, Literary Review, London Magazine*. He has published four collections; his latest publication *Words Take Me* (Lapwing Press) appeared in February 2013. He lives in York.

Yvie Holder's poems draw on politics, childhood, loss, landscape and her UK and Caribbean heritage. She has been published online, in anthologies, and commended in the York Literature Festival Competition.

Andy Humphrey has won numerous prizes and runs the 'open mic' night Speakers' Corner in York, which has featured hundreds of performers since 2006. His poetry collections include *A Long Way to Fall* (2013) and *Satires* (2015).

Will Kemp has won the Keats-Shelley Prize, the Envoi International, the Debut Collection Award and the Cinnamon Pamphlet Competition. Cinnamon has published his collections *Nocturnes*, *Lowland*, T*he Painters Who Studied Clouds* and his award-winning pamphlet, *The Missing Girl*.

Pauline Kirk was born in Birmingham, and moved to York in 2002. After receiving an Arts Council 'New Beginning Award', she gave up her day job with Leeds Social Services to become a full-time writer and editor. Ten collections of her poetry and six novels have been published, three written with her daughter as PJ Quinn. She is editor of Fighting Cock Press, and on the editorial board of *Dream Catcher* magazine.

Peter Knaggs is currently the Writer in Residence at Sirius Academy West, in Hull. He is the author of *Cowboy Hat* and *You're So Vain You Probably Think This Book Is About You*. A new collection, *Shiznit*, is forthcoming from Wrecking Ball Press.

Gill Lambert is a poet and teacher from Yorkshire. She won the 2016 Ilkley Literature Festival Open mic competition and runs the regular *Shaken in Sheeptown* events in Skipton. Gill's first solo pamphlet will be published by Indigo Dreams in 2017, followed by a full collection with Stairwell in 2018.

Patrick Lodge was born in Wales, lives in Yorkshire and travels on an Irish passport. His poetry has been published widely in journals and magazines, including *Envoi*, *Ink, Sweat & Tears* and *Mediterranean Poetry*. He was the winner of the 2015 Blackwater International Poetry Competition. His collections *An Anniversary of Flight* (2013) and *Shenanigans* (2016) were published by Valley Press.

Char March has won many awards for poetry, playwrighting and short fiction. Her credits include: the short story collection *Something Vital Fell Through* (2013*)*, five poetry collections including *The Thousand Natural Shocks* (2011), six BBC Radio 4 plays, and seven stage plays.

Fokkina McDonnell is a psychotherapist in Manchester. Her poems have been broadcast and published in a range of anthologies and magazines, including *Magma*, *Orbis*, *Mslexia* and *The North*, as well as commended or placed in poetry competitions. Fokkina's debut collection *Another Life* was published by Oversteps Books at the end of 2016.

Andrew McMillan was born in South Yorkshire in 1988. His debut collection *physical* was published in 2015; it has won numerous awards including The Guardian First Book Award and a Somerset Maugham Award, and was shortlisted for The Dylan Thomas Prize and the Costa Poetry Award. He lives in Manchester.

Ian McMillan is a poet, journalist and broadcaster. He is well known to Yorkshire audiences from his many appearances at festivals, schools and arts centres throughout the county. He is presenter of BBC Radio 3's *The Verb* and author of many books, including *Talking Myself Home* (2008) and *To Fold the Evening Star: New and Selected Poems* (2016).

Rob Miles's poetry has appeared widely in magazines and anthologies such as *Ambit, Orbis, The Interpreter's House, York Literary Review, South Bank Poetry, The Anthology of Age* and *The Anthology of Love* (The Emma Press), and *Remembering Oluwale* (Valley Press). He's won competitions including the Philip Larkin Prize (2014), and the Resurgence Prize (2016). Other poems have been commended or shortlisted in competitions including the Bridport, Gregory O'Donoghue, and the National Poetry Competition.

Pete Morgan (1939 – 2010) was a poet and broadcaster who lived in Robin Hood's Bay, York and Beverley, among other places. He was an inventive and exciting poet and a masterful reader/performer. His full-length collections included *A Winter Visitor* (Martin, Secker & Warburg 1983), set in Robin Hood's Bay, and *August Light* (Arc 2005), a gathering of later work which, sadly, turned out to be valedictory.

Helen Mort was born in Sheffield. Her first collection *Division Street* (2013) won the Fenton Aldeburgh Prize. Her collection *No Map Could Show Them* (2016) is a Poetry Book Society Recommendation.

Paul Munden worked as creative writing tutor in adult education and for various universities, before becoming Director of NAWE (National Association of Writers in Education). He received an Eric Gregory Award in 1987. His collections include *Analogue/Digital* (Smith / Doorstop 2015). He is the editor of *Feeling the Pressure: Poetry and Science of Climate Change* (British Council 2008).

James Nash was born in London in 1949, and has been a resident of Leeds since 1971. He is a well-known provider of creative writing workshops in schools, universities and the community, and is regularly called on as a host of literary events. His most recent collection of poetry is *Some Things Matter: 63 Sonnets* (2012), and he collaborated with Matthew Hedley Stoppard on *Cinema Stories* (2015).

Marie Naughton grew up in Harrogate and went to school in York. She now lives in Manchester and works as a psychotherapist. Her poems have appeared widely in magazines and anthologies in the UK and Ireland, and she is working on a first collection. She won the Cafe Writers competition in 2012.

Ian Parks was born in 1959 in Mexborough. He is the author of eight collections of poems, the most recent of which was a Poetry Book Society Choice. He was writer-in-residence at Gladstone's Library in 2012 and Writing Fellow at De Monfort University, Leicester from 2012-2014. *Citizens* is due from Smokestack Books in 2017.

Stuart Pickford is married with three children. He teaches at a local school in Harrogate. His latest book is *Swimming with Jellyfish* (2016), published by Smith/Doorstop.

Robert Powell lives in York. He has published three collections of poetry; *Harvest of Light* (Stone Flower, 2007), *All* (Valley Press, 2015), and *A Small Box of River*, a collaborative artist's book and exhibition with Jake Attree (2016). He was the winner of the 2012 Elmet Prize judged by Kathleen Jamie, and his poems and stories have appeared in *Bridport: The Winners (2010), Dreamcatcher, Orbis* and *The Rialto*, as well as numerous Canadian journals.

Clare Pollard has published several collections of poetry with Bloodaxe, including *Changeling* (2011), *Ovid's Heroines* (2013) and *Incarnation* (2017).

Wendy Pratt was born in Scarborough in 1978. Her work has been widely published in journals and magazines and has featured in several anthologies, including *The Forward Anthology* and *The Emergency Poet.* She has a pamphlet and a full collection with Prolebooks, a pamphlet with Flarestack Poets and her latest full collection, *Gifts the Mole Gave Me* is being published by Valley Press in October 2017. She is currently working on a creative writing PhD with Hull University.

D A Prince's first pamphlet, *Undoing Time*, was published by Pikestaff Press in 1998, followed by *Keeping in touch* from the same publisher in 2002. Meanwhile Manifold Century Chapbooks had brought out *Without Boundaries* in 2001. In 2008 Happenstance Press published her full-length collection, *Nearly the Happy Hour*; this was the first full-length publication from this lively publisher. *Common Ground*, also from HappenStance Press, was published in 2014. This collection won the East Midlands Book Award 2015.

Lesley Quayle is a widely published, prize-winning poet, former editor of Leeds-based poetry magazine *Aireings* and a folk/blues singer, who lived for over thirty years in Yorkshire; in Leeds and then Starbotton. Her chapbook, *Songs for Lesser Gods*, about the foot and mouth crisis was published by erbacce in 2009, and her most recent collection *Sessions* was published by Indigo Dreams in 2013.

Bethany Rivers' debut pamphlet, *Off The Wall* (2016) was published by Indigo Dreams Publishing. She has had poems published by *Envoi, Cinnamon Press, Blithe Spirit* and *Ink Sweat & Tears*, amongst others. She was born and brought up in Leeds, where her mother still lives. She teaches creative writing, mentors writers of novels and autobiographies, and runs poetry healing retreats.

Carol Rowntree Jones won the inaugural Overton Poetry Prize with her pamphlet *This Is Not Normal Behaviour*, published by Lamplight Press. Her work has also appeared in *The North, Staple, Assent* and *111O*. She has a chapbook out with Dancing Girl Press in the US.

Miles Salter lives in York. His poetry collections are *The Border* (2011) and *Animals* (2013), both published by Valley Press. His other writing includes journalism and fiction for children and Young Adults. He has an M.A. in Creative Writing from York St John University.

Peter Sansom runs, with his wife Ann, The Poetry Business and Smith / Doorstop publishers. He has led countless workshops and continues to edit *The North*. His collections include *Careful What You Wish For* (Carcanet, 2015) and *Selected Poems* (Carcanet, 2010).

John Siddique is the author of six books, the most recent of which is *Full Blood*. His work has featured in many places, including *Granta, The Guardian, Poetry Review* and BBC Radio 4. *The Spectator* refers to him as 'A stellar British poet.' *The Times of India* calls him 'Rebellious by nature, pure at heart.' John is a Fellow of the Royal Society of Arts, and is a former Royal Literary Fund Fellow at York St. John University.

Michael Shann was born and grew up in Otley and now lives in Walthamstow, north-east London, where he is a member of Forest Poets. He has published two books with Paekakariki Press, *Euphrasy* and *Walthamstow.* Michael works as Head of Membership and Volunteering at Carers UK and has coordinated the charity's creative writing competition for the past three years.

Jane Sharp lives near Barnsley. She is author of the novel *Tears From the Sun - A Cretan Journey,* and has published A *Poet's Year in Glenridding*, *From Maths to Making Tea*, and T*he Horta Pickers*. Her poems have been broadcast on BBC Radio and have featured in various magazines.

Hannah Stone has an MA in creative writing from Leeds Trinity University. *Lodestone* was published in 2016 and *Missing Miles* is forthcoming in 2017. She performs throughout Yorkshire and beyond.

Matthew Hedley Stoppard was appointed the first official Otley Town Poet in 2016. He has two collections published by Valley Press, and his poems have featured in magazines, anthologies and on radio.

Nick Toczek has worked as a poet, journalist, musician, lyricist and broadcaster. His poetry collections with MacMillan in the 1990s made him a best-selling children's writer. His first political book *Haters, Baiters and Would-Be Dictators: Anti-Semitism and the UK Far-Right*, was published by Routledge at the end of 2015.

Sarah Wallis is a poet and playwright based in Leeds. Recently published by *Flight Journal* and *all the sins*, and in the forthcoming anthology *Watermarks, for Lido Lovers & Wild Swimmers* by The Frogmore Papers. She has held residencies at West Yorkshire Playhouse and Harrogate Theatre, which have supported and developed her plays *Laridae* and *The Rain King*. She also co-curates Leeds Pub Theatre with the playwright Jonathan Hall.

Mike Watts is a writer/spoken-word artist from Hull. He has performed at festivals and venues around the UK, including the Edinburgh Fringe. He is the author of three collections of poetry: *Coming to a street near you* (Night Publishing), *Day and night in the damaged goods factory* (Burning Eye), *Jawbreaker* (Paul Gibson Publishing), and his fourth collection is to be released by Wrecking Ball Press in August 2017.

Fiona Ritchie Walker has read on BBC Radio 4's *Poetry Please.* Her poem, *After Diagnosis*, won first prize in the 2015 Carers UK poetry competition. Her poetry collections include *The Second Week of the Soap* (Red Squirrel Press) and *Lip Reading* (Diamond Twig).

Acknowledgments

Helen Boden's 'The Gallery Tour Pauses in Front of Simon Armitage's Portrait' refers to the portrait *Simon Armitage* by Paul Wright, which was in the BP portrait award 2014.

Pat Borthwick's 'Hare' was first published in *The Road I Take* (Pharos Press, 2016).

Jo Brandon's 'Town Hall Steps, Leeds' was first published as part of the Leads to Leeds project.

Carole Bromley's 'The Stonegate Devil' was first published in the collection of the same name by Smith/Doorstop, 2015.

Michael Brown's 'Sheffield' was first published in *The Moth*, and subsequently in his pamphlet *Locations for a Soul* (Templar Poetry, 2016).

Anne Caldwell's 'Nidderdale' first appeared in *Woven Landscapes* (Avalanche Press, 2016), edited by Deborah Gaye.

Becky Cherriman's 'Christchurch, Ilkley' was first published in *Envoi*, Issue 170, ed. Kay Syrad, and subsequently in her first collection *Empires of Clay* (Cinnamon Press, 2016).

David Coldwell's 'The Moor' is from his pamphlet *Flowers by the Road* (Templar Poetry, 2017).

Oliver Comins' 'York Ghosts' was first published in *The North* 53 (2014).

Joey Connolly's 'Chekhov's Gun' has previously appeared in *Poems In Which*, *Best British Poetry 2014* (Salt) and *The Sunday Times*, as well as *Long Pass* (Carcanet).

Julia Deakin's 'Boar Lane, Leeds' was first published in *Pennine Platform* Issue 73 (Summer 2013).

Janet Dean's 'Brian Jones' was first published online by Clear Poetry in July 2016.

Carol Ann Duffy's 'Telephoning Home' is from *New Selected Poems* (Picador, 2004). Copyright © Carol Ann Duffy. Reproduced by permission of the author c/o Rogers, Coleridge & White Ltd., 20 Powis Mews, London, W11 1JN.

Ian Duhig's 'Nothing Pie' was first published in *The Bloodaxe Book of 20th Century Poetry* (ed. Edna Longley, 2000).

Antony Dunn's 'Suburban' was first published in *Take This One to Bed* (Valley Press, 2016).

Mike Farren's 'York Street Furniture, 1981' is from his pamphlet *Pierrot and his mother* (Templar Poetry, 2017).

Dave Gough's 'A Yorkshire Alphabet' was first published in *Aesthetica*, 2004.

Cora Greenhill's 'Seen in Sheffield' was first published in *The Sheffield Anthology* (Smith Doorstop, 2012), and subsequently in her collection *The Point of Waking* (Oversteps Books ,2013).

Yvie Holder's 'Surviving the Prince of Wales' was first published in her pamphlet *Abolition Blues and Other Poems* (2014).

Andy Humphrey's 'Nobody Hurries in Harrogate' was the winner of the Rhyming Verse category in the Northampton Literature Group Open Poetry Competition, 2009, and was first published on the Group's website. It subsequently appeared in his collection *Satires* (Stairwell Books, 2015).

Will Kemp's 'Fountains Abbey' was first published on *The Guardian*'s website in 2009.

Pauline Kirk's 'Family Group at York Station' was first published in *Pennine Platform.*

Peter Knaggs' 'Hull' was first published in *You're So Vain You Probably Think This Book is About You* (Wrecking Ball Press, 2015).

Patrick Lodge's 'Mary Bateman's Lament' was first published in *Shenanigans* (Valley Press, 2016).

Rob Miles's 'An Opening at the Mill' was first published in *Angle*, Spring 2015.

Pete Morgan's 'Brinks' was first published in *A Winter Visitor* by Secker & Warburg, 1983.

Helen Mort's 'Lowedges' is from her collection *Division Street*, published by Chatto & Windus. Reprinted by permission of The Random House Group Ltd. © Helen Mort 2013.

Paul Munden's 'The Riverside Arms' was first published in *Feeling the pressure: Poetry and science of climate change* (British Council, 2008) and subsequently in *Analogue/Digital* (Smith/Doorstop, 2015).

Clare Pollard's 'Whitby' is from her collection *Changeling* (Bloodaxe Books, 2011).

D A Prince's 'Heading North' was first published in *The 11th Ware Poetry Competition Anthology 2009.*

Peter Sansom's 'Shalesmoor, Sheffield' is from his collection *Careful What You Wish For* (Carcanet, 2015).